Dedications

For Zoe, my beautiful and smart daughter, my heart and soul.

For my gone but never forgotten father, Tony Ciambro, who will awe and inspire me until the day I die. "He fought the good fight, he finished the race, he kept the faith."

For my mom, who taught me to never leave the house without make-up. I miss her.

Preface

This book has two purposes. One, on a surface level, to make you laugh, think, and be more considerate. And secondly, on a deeper level, to help normal and quasi-normal people identify crazy, keep crazy out of their lives, and know they're not crazy.

I have 33 years experience as a therapist. I have a master's degree in counseling and education, and five licensures in chemical dependency, mental health, and teaching. I've seen and heard it all (almost).

After thousands of hours of continuing education, workshops, symposiums by published therapists, spiritual leaders, attorneys, and doctors, I've decided that I have as much to say about life, therapy, what works, and what doesn't as they do because I probably have had as many or more clients and practical counseling experience than some of them.

My family, friends, and colleagues have encouraged me to write this book for years, and now I have the confidence to do so.

Bullshit 101

Bigger and Better!

(a self-help book for normal
and quasi-normal people)

Patricia A. Ciambro
MS, LICDC, LPC

Edited by Ron Siemer

ISBN-13: 978-0-9964129-1-9

Visit www.bs101book.com

Cover design by Kyra A. Siemer

Edited by Ron Siemer

Acknowledgements

Thank you to my incredible friends and family who are my collaborators. The dearest ones were acknowledged in the first edition of this book.

This version gives a special acknowledgment to the memory of one of my best friends and editor, Ron Siemer, who passed away on February 25th, 2017. He had been one of the best friends that I could ever hope for, and a wonderful godfather to my daughter, Zoe. Both books would have never happened without him. Thank you, Ron. Without our endless hours of philosophizing, dissecting, laughing, and debating, this book would never have materialized. It has been a wonderful life journey with you.

Finally, thank you to April Barnswell for formatting this book for me.

I have the best friends in the world!

Table of Contents

1

Ethics Patrol

When you see people doing bad things, you should nail them, confront them, or correct them.

It's okay to be assertive.

There are two exceptions. If it is your boss or a drug dealer, then you should remain an anonymous whistleblower so you don't get fired or killed.

2

No One Likes a Whiner

If you whine, no one will like you. Then you won't have any friends. Then you'll be depressed because no one likes you and you don't have any friends.

3

Dogs and Pills
Can Be Great Therapy

If you are lonely and depressed, you should get a dog — if you are capable of taking care of it. Dogs are always happy to see you; and if you walk them, you will have actual social contact with other human beings, especially if you have a cute dog! And if you get a rescue dog, you can feel even better about yourself.

If that doesn't work, you might need medication, because your brain chemistry doesn't work quite right. See a psychiatrist, because they know about brain chemistry (family doctors don't). If he/she prescribes the proper antidepressant or other drugs, take it as prescribed. Otherwise, you are wasting time and money, or you are a prescription drug addict.

4

Be Careful With Whom You Procreate

You would think that this title is obvious to every human. But most of us normal or quasi-normal people know that is not true. Sometimes the family history of craziness, obesity, stupidity, bad genetics, and addictions isn't obvious at first. That's why you should teach your kids about analyzing the family history of someone they will marry and/or procreate with one day. And look very deep into that history.

For example, maybe at first you thought your future significant other's family were just heavy social drinkers and like to party. Then, later (after you have reproduced), you realize they are a bunch of alcoholics. Now you most likely have passed that genetic predisposition on to your kids. The same goes for mental and physical diseases.

Please pick a good mating partner so as to increase the probability that humans will evolve in a healthy direction and the bad eggs will die off.

CRAZY + CRAZY ≠ NORMAL

5

LA LA LA LA LA
(Magical Thinking)

Some people hate REALITY. They drift off and fantasize about people, places, and things they don't have. Get a f****ing grip and deal with what you've got. Maybe you just need to raise the bar, get a better job, find a more stable partner, get sober, or whatever. But stop fantasizing about stuff that's not doable.

6

You Would Have Been Better Off Raised by Wolves

People that were abused (sexually, emotionally, physically, spiritually, etc.) should NEVER EVER feel guilty (and they often do). Instead they should spit on their abusers' graves. And find wonderful, positive, kind, and mentally healthy people to emulate.

7

Your Bad Karma Is Putting Up with Assholes

(or, clinically stated, personality disorders)

What doesn't kill you will make you stronger. There are some people in your life that you need to detach from, ignore, or just plain run away from because they are toxic to your well-being. I repeat, "DETACH, IGNORE, OR RUN AWAY." If that's not feasible because they live with you, or you work with them, or you are forced to socialize with them, or if every conversation becomes an altercation, just don't talk to them whenever possible. Take a vow of silence.

The people (assholes) that I'm referring to are the kinds with personality disorders, like Paranoid,

Schizoid, Schizotypal, Antisocial, Borderline, Histri-onic, Narcissistic, Avoidant, Dependent, and Obses-sive-Compulsive. There are volumes written about these sorts of people. Google any of the above-men-tioned personality disorders, and you'll say, "So, that's what's wrong with so and so?"

8

Beware of Jealous

Of course, when people are jealous of you, you should be flattered. However, jealousy is evil. Jealous people want to have what you have and sometimes go to great evil lengths to try and get it.

I heard it put succinctly by the character Roger Sterling on Mad Men. The line went something like, "You spend your whole life building something, and then people get jealous and try to take it away from you."

Jealous people enjoy seeing you miserable. Jealous people will never genuinely like you. So don't try changing them, or try to be friends with them, or sucking up in any form. That is an exercise in futility.

Keep your distance from jealous people (any one of them could be a Borderline Personality Disorder in disguise). There's a fine line between jealousy and Borderlines. Both are bad and disruptive to your life.

9

Real Parenting

Parenting is tough. Why do parents decide to slack off parenting when their kids get to be teenagers through 20-somethings? This is the time you have to be vigilant about being a parent. This is when you have to spy on their e-mails, go through their belongings looking for weed, eavesdropping on their phone calls, etc..., to make sure they are going to grow up to be responsible people. Such vigilance is unnecessary if your kids are perfect and listen to love, reasoning, and rational thought.

I know only one set of parents with perfect kids. They instill what the mom calls the 5 R's: 1) Respectfulness, 2) Responsibility, 3) Resilience, 4) Resourcefulness, and 5) Reliability.

And guess what? Kids' brains are not fully developed for executive functioning until about age 27. That means they can't really make an adult decision until then. And we let them drive at 16! So, at the first inkling of them spinning out of control, you have only what I call the 5C's for leverage. They are: 1) Computer, 2) Cell phone, 3) Car, 4) Cash, and 5) Credit Card.

Take these things away and watch how fast your kids will respond or pretend to respond to your parenting requests. Slowly give these things back as they start to show progress.

All parenting is bribery (clinicians like to call it *positive reinforcement*). Don't you start giving your children choices when they are little — i.e., "Max, would you like spinach or carrots?" They are duped into a choice that you like. Then you say, "If you finish all your carrots, you can have ice cream." And when they get bigger, the bribes just get more costly — i.e., "If you really want a car, first you go to rehab!" Bribery and dupery!

10

Weirdo Homeschoolers

In my mind and experience there are only four reasons to homeschool your kids (I am still a licensed teacher).

1) You are traveling around the world for a year with your kids (those chances are slim to none for most of us mortals).

2) You live in a horrible neighborhood with really horrible schools, and you can't afford to send them to private schools (you probably would have moved if that was the situation).

3) Your child is a famous child star.

4) You are a weirdo fundamentalist (choose any religion) who doesn't want your children to be tainted

by REALITY!!!

Let me expound on the fourth reason. You do not care that your kids might learn negotiation and coping skills by interacting with peers and teachers whom they do not like or get along with in a real school. A real school might prepare them for the bad bosses and horrible co-workers that they will work with some day.

It's true that in a good school day you might actually get only four hours of academics, but real school teaches us to get along with other people, how to be teased without decomposing, when to shut up, when to run, when to fight, and a lot of other life skills.

I love hearing home-schooling parents say, "My children (even weirder, my teenagers) are in play groups, sports, etc..., with other home-schooled kids." The parents have chosen the niche for their "reality-isolated" kids, and if they don't like that group, then they will find another group that suits the parent. That doesn't happen in real school.

And do these homeschooling parents really know AP (advanced placement) English, trig, chemistry,

Spanish, etc...??????? NO! They just think that on-
line learning can really replace an expert teacher
who might be an inspiration to your little darling —
or who might be Attila the Hun and teach them to
have good coping skills to negotiate this sometimes
harsh world. Amen.

11

Guilt Is Good

If you feel guilty about something, you probably are. You should sincerely apologize, learn from your mistakes, and don't do it again. People need to feel guilty for doing stupid or shameful things. Otherwise, we would have anarchy and a bunch of sociopaths running things. The exception is when guilt is not warranted because you were abused and felt like it was your fault and you deserved it. That's f***'d up.

There is a difference between guilt and shame. Guilt is "I made a mistake." And shame is "I am a mistake." No one should feel shame, but guilt—yes.

12

Manners and Such Should Be Introduced in 1st Grade

I am positive that if Manners 101, Banking 101, and Comparative Religions 101 were introduced in the 1st grade, we would have a more peaceful, sane, and financially responsible world.

Children, teenagers, and young adults appear ruder and less socially acceptable than they were 20-30 years ago. I can gauge this because I have occasionally substitute taught for the last 10 years in the same school system. (I have maintained a teaching license for the past 43 years and use it once in a while.) I also counsel kids once in awhile. I prefer adults. The point is that kids have definitely deteriorated in the manners department. My teacher friends agree.

Credit card debt is out of control in the U.S. In Banking 101, we could teach kids how to save money, not spend more than they earn, and there's always a rainy day. These are real skills that would teach them to remain fiscally sound throughout their lives. And don't have children until you know you can save for their college or vocational school fund!

Teaching comparative religions would teach kids to be more tolerant of other cultures and learn more history – because religion is history. Maybe they would grow up without the prejudiced idea that "my religion is better than your religion." If all countries in the world taught this, we might be able to achieve world peace. I know this is utopian thinking, but we have to start somewhere.

I observe people becoming more "fundamentalist" in their thinking. This is SO bat-shit crazy!

13

Borderlines Are the Worst

Borderline Personality Disorders make Narcissistic Personality Disorders look good. Narcissistic-personality-disordered people are just plain self-absorbed and don't give a shit about anyone else. Borderlines act as if they give a shit and always need human targets.

Borderlines would like to destroy their targets emotionally, and sometimes physically, but are afraid of going to prison. Such a person always needs an ENEMY. He/she has fun seeing how many allies he/she can get against the perceived enemy. Usually the enemy is a former friend or a relative who didn't fulfill the Borderline's self-absorbed desires.

Like vicious SNAKES, Borderlines turn on these

people by manipulating and lying profusely about their targeted enemies. Borderlines like to watch and proliferate the destruction of their enemies' jobs, relationships, money, or anything that is dear to them. This is a real power trip. And when they don't succeed, they move on to the new targets.

It usually takes a while for the innocent ones to notice this is happening to them.

Be very wary of people who don't have close long-time friends. They probably have some kind of personality disorder, especially Borderlines. There is a good reason they don't have long-term close friends: they have burnt their bridges and are looking for new enemies or targets. Both Borderlines and Narcissists can be extremely charming. Thank goodness for the stupid ones; you can see them coming.

There is little therapeutic help for these personality disorders. So, as previously stated in another chapter: "Run away, detach and/or ignore them."

14

Incongruity (people talking out of both sides of their mouths)

According to my *Webster's Dictionary* the word "incongruous" means:

1) made of disparate, inconsistent, or discordant parts or qualities

2) not consistent with what is logical, usual, or correct

3) inappropriate. Ergo, an incongruous person might also be called a hypocrite — or a politician.

Have a conviction and stick to it — if it's NOT a stupid conviction!

15

Narcissistic New

Narcissists come in all shapes and sizes; men out-number women 4-1. This personality disorder oc-curs in 6 to 8% of the general population.

If you are a person that always wants new stuff so you can be envied, you are probably an empty nar-cissist. If you have been called an asshole multiple times in your life, then you are probably a narcis-sist. But a narcissist does not ever recognize this in himself, so he would be in denial. And he would also blame other people for his depression, rage, and lack of friends. But if, after you read this and you conclude that you're not a narcissist, you're probably thinking, "I know so many of them!"

Here is an example of my phrase "narcissistic new."

You are not a multi-millionaire or a billionaire, and you bought a new car, and 2 to 3 years later you want a better one. Or you want a new girlfriend/ boyfriend, and you are married. Or you are often fantasizing about the next best thing—spouse, car, house, big-ticket item. Then you get it, the void is only temporarily filled, and then you're on to the next fantasy/fix that, of course, will fail or not fulfill.

When the temporary happiness is gone, it's always someone else's fault. And if you rage (there's a huge difference between anger and rage) when criticized, you are an asshole narcissist. But you won't recognize that you are a narcissist because of your denial, lack of insight, and rationalizing.

16

F'cked-Up People
Create Chaos

Cheating spouses, ISIS, self-absorbed assholes, and jealous, stupid, and greedy personality disorders all create chaos, pandemonium, and havoc.

Their messes usually have to be cleaned up by normal and quasi-normal people.

Do not confuse being animated, gregarious, humorous, interesting, and having a big personality, with the traits of drama kings and queens.

Drama kings and queens need chaos for some kind of a weird rush or cheap thrill. Most are probably sexually frustrated, impotent, or frigid and need to rationalize their bad behavior and make others seem like the "bad guys." Narcissists and Borderline personality disorders really like to create chaos and screw up relationships.

There are also quiet but crazy people. They are mostly passive-aggressive and sneaky.

17

Sex Is Free and So Is Welfare

Why aren't we passing out birth control for free? It's very cheap. People should not procreate until they've saved for college or vocational school before the kid or kids are born.

But I also have seen enormous high-end welfare in the form of government jobs. I worked for 10 years as a civilian substance abuse counselor for the Department of Defense. I saw a lot more waste and abuse than just people abusing drugs and alcohol. Every politician should be required to work as a GS-11 or below before holding office to learn how we squander government money.

Do you know what "fallout" money is? Every year,

every federal office (DOD, DOE, DOJ, etc...) has to spend the full amount of money budgeted for that office before September 30th (the end of the fiscal year) or lose that appropriated money for the next year. So whether it's needed or not, often highly-paid department heads must spend $$$ on sometimes outrageously expensive and unnecessary stuff. I had to do it in my office one year. Remember Gov. Sarah Palin's "Bridge to Nowhere?" — and the $800 toilet seats?

This chapter has nothing to do with self–help. But it points to a twisted mindset of the government. I do know many brilliant, competent people who have worked for the government. We just need to find more of them.

18

If You Need Hearing Aids, Wear Them!

Stop annoying people who can hear because you can't and won't wear hearing aids! If you need glasses you wear them – don't you?

19

Always Be Appropriate

Always be appropriate.

If you don't want people to think you are crazy, then always be appropriate. By appropriate, I mean always adhere to "normal" societal norms. Being appropriate is not that difficult. You control your temper, especially in public. You should have impeccable manners and be civil.

There is good crazy and bad crazy. Good crazy is a little eccentric and quirky, and you don't do bizarre and bad things to other people. Bad crazy is acting like a lunatic, being an asshole and deceitful.

Let's act more like the residents of Downton Abbey than Donald Trump.

20

Be Old-Fashioned! Send Birthday Cards

Send birthday cards to people you care about — not stupid email cards (lame) or text (lamer) or FB (lamest) unless you are the busiest person on Earth. For a person important to you, make an effort to buy a card, address an envelope, send it on time, and keep a birthday book of dates of peoples' birthdays that you care about. Otherwise, you are probably just lazy and/or not motivated.

The same goes for thank-you notes.

21

Destination Weddings

Unless all your family and friends are multimillion-aires, destination weddings are bullshit.

Are you so narcissistic that you think people want to spend thousands of dollars on airfare, hotels, rental cars, and a large gift to see you get married???!!!

Most people enjoy attending weddings, but not when it's costing them the price of a nice used car.

If you are getting married for the 2nd, 3rd, or 4th time, and your friends just want to get away and party with you, then a destination wedding is acceptable.

But the invitation should say something like, "Do you want to go on an expensive vacation with us

(and watch us get married)?" "No need to RSVP—
just show up at Sandals in Negril, Jamaica on Janu-
ary 1, 20--."

22

Couples Therapy

If you have gone from love to contempt, do not bother with couples therapy. It's a waste of time and money.

My observation of a doomed relationship is this continuum: Love → annoyance → dislike → hatred → contempt.

If you don't nip it in the bud between annoyance and dislike, it's over! There is no going back to a good relationship after dislike. And that's when couples usually seek therapy.

Find a good attorney instead.

23

"God Is Fair and Nobody Gets It All"

My sister's friend Doreen always used that line, and I quote her often. When I facilitated intensive outpatient substance abuse groups I used to write on the chalkboard, for openers, "Life is a series of cumulative losses." — the point of which was, "get used to it."

The older we get, the more losses we have — i.e., loved ones, stocks, youth, etc.... Grief is the appropriate response. But some people whine or drink or drug such losses away, magically thinking about something else. Try to be the nicest (not sappy), funniest, most honest, and most productive person you can be. You can actually do this, and (I'm told) it makes you feel wonderfully accomplished.

24

Overachievers

Psychologists say that the overachieving mentality is the same as the underachieving mentality. I think that is bullshit. True, both might be neurotic. But would you want to overachieve or underachieve in this life? If you answered underachieve, then you really are a loser.

Because overachievers are perfectionists, they must be careful that their OCD traits do not get in the way of relationships. My advice to overachievers (and kudos to them) is, "Don't screw up your personal relationships."

Overachievers always do well in their jobs and careers.

Underachievers screw up most things because they're lazy.

25

The Art of Conversation

I believe that, thanks to computers, we have created an entire younger generation of people who cannot converse for more than 1.5 minutes, punctuate, or spell without the use of a spell-check or grammar-check algorithm. And cursive writing is almost obsolete.

I know teachers who have taught for more than 30 years, and they will tell you we have almost induced ADHD (attention deficit hyperactivity disorder) into kids who didn't already have it because they need and want to be perpetually stimulated by some kind of electronic device. They need to move their thumbs spastically and fingers all the time (texting, gaming, etc...). It's the new tick! To merely listen to a teacher or professor lecture is too painful for their short attention spans and electronically anesthetized brains. And forget conversing; that's too much trouble. They would rather text or Facebook phrases to one another.

Complete sentences, spelling, and punctuation are important. Why? Because actual conversation with a real live human being can be fun, difficult, boring, intellectually stimulating, angering, frustrating, and full of all kinds of human emotions that make us introspective, engaged, and interested in other people's lives – that is, more balanced and less selfish.

But if this task of conversing is too daunting, then at least ACT as if you're interested. If that's too much trouble, then you'll probably end up spending a lot of time on the computer with superficial friends who really don't gave a shit about you.

26

If You Don't Have a To-Do List, You Don't Have Enough Sh*t To Do

(Written by my daughter, Zoe)

One of the greatest life skills I learned from my mother was the power and benefit of creating a daily 'to-do' list. Even if it's a lazy Sunday or there's not much going on, we all have at least a few things needing accomplished each day, and having a 'to-do' list is a testament to you being a responsible person with a good work ethic and the ability to stick to a deadline and/or not procrastinate.

If you don't have a daily or even weekly to-do list which is regularly updated, then I can only conclude that you must not have enough shit to do. And if you really have so little going on in your life that you have found no reason to buy a calendar or a stack of sticky-notes, then logically you must fall into at one of these categories:

1) Between the ages of 0-14 years old

2) Stoner that lives in their enabling parents' basement

3) Drug addict that lives in the street

4) Negligent parent

5) Jobless with an enabling significant other (or parents)

6) About to be jobless (because you don't make to-do lists)

7) In prison

8) Slave/indentured servant

There's a second, arguably even worse, explanation for why one does not have an ever-evolving 'to-do' list: You have a lot to do, but you're a disorganized, chaotic mess. In this case, although you may be intelligent, congenial, and possess the desire to be active, you probably experience a lot of frustration and unexplained failure due to your disorganization.

The bottom line is this: Success in anything is 50% showing up, 10% actual talent, and 40% organization (yes, I just made that up). Creating a daily to-do list is tantamount in getting on the organization-bandwagon, and it also helps you to reflect back upon what you've actually done with your life over the past day, week, and year. If your life is truly so routine or disorganized that you don't write down daily tasks, maybe it's time for a reality check and some therapy.

27

Rubber-Band Therapy

I do not know who thought of rubber-band thera-py, but I have advised clients to do it. It is a short-term, easy fix for obsessive or negative thoughts that won't leave your head alone. Here it is: put a thick rubber band on your wrist, and every time you think a contemptuous or worrisome thought about an ex-spouse, finances, a bad boss, a so-called friend, or anything that is eating up much of your think-ing during the day, just SNAP that rubber band as hard as you can and the pain will snap that negative thought away. You might have to snap it a hundred times a day to stop thinking the obtrusive thought you don't want.

After many broken rubber bands and bruised wrists, you might be cured (at least for a short while)! But don't be a wimp about snapping it hard or it won't be effective!

28

Loyalty Is the Rock of Gibraltar

Loyalty is not a plastic card you get at the grocery store or gas station. It seems real loyalty is a lost art. Loyalty to family, spouses, friends, jobs, etc..., is one of the most important character traits or virtues.

Loyal people are like loyal dogs. They are committed to other people through thick and thin. Loyal people don't cheat, lie, steal, or do sneaky things to their friends, family or co-workers. Loyal people tend to be happier because they have long-standing friends. Beware of people who do not have long-lasting friendships! They generally are not loyal or committed. Disloyalty is treason. The loss of someone's loyalty destroys confidence. And disloyalty will destroy a business, relationships, friend-ships, and families. Loyalty is a life-sustaining part of any worthwhile and healthy relationship. Disloy-al people are more like snakes than dogs!

29

High Tolerance for the Bizarre

Putting up with bad behavior from other people for very long periods of time can be detrimental to anyone's good mental health. It's like building a tolerance for alcohol — not a good thing.

30

No Man Is an Island

People who live alone tend to get weird. By weird I mean they forget or want to forget how to interact or converse with other humans. They'd rather talk to their cats, dogs, or fish; they don't talk back. And people who live in the boonies alone get even weirder — e.g., the Unibomber. And a loner really doesn't like feedback from others either, because people might tell him that he is weird or an asshole.

So if you live alone, have lots of crazy dinner parties and house guests, and go out and socialize. Telephone friends just to let them know you're thinking of them. Invite people over for coffee or a simple meal or meet them somewhere for a beer.

And occasionally look at your own lifestyle. If you

discover that you have accrued more animals or guns than might be considered normal, look out! That's a really good sign that you might be acting crazy. Prove that you're sane and healthy by changing that goofy behavior!

31

A Fool at 40
Is a Fool Forever

I love that idiom. "A Fool at 40 is a Fool Forever," could also be stated as "An asshole remains an asshole forever" or "Stupid begets stupid."

Scientists say that our brains should be ready for "executive functioning" around age 27 (ADHD folks take longer). But I think we have all observed adults who never grew up, or regress when under stress, or whine like children, or keep making poor decisions and mistakes over and over.

These things can mostly be attributed to personality disorders. I cannot say this enough—people with personality disorders are the ones who f'ck up the

world and relationships by making bad decisions
and destroying things.

Fools forever.

32

The Blame Game

If you rationalize, justify, and/or blame your bad behavior on someone else, you likely will be an asshole all your life. If you cannot be accountable for your bad decisions and continue to blame people, places, and things for your misery, you will not be a happy camper no matter where or how you camp. Get your head out of your butt and get some insight into your crippled personality and habits. This is called building character and becoming a nice person. A side effect is noticing that you have a crowd of great friends who can and do enrich your life!

33

Bitching vs. Whining

Bitching is therapeutic venting. I am honored when someone calls me a bitch because it's evidence that I didn't take his or her bullshit or stupid sob story or accept bad customer service. Bitching also is warranted when someone has screwed something up and you need to unscrew it.

Whining is self-pity, meaning you want others to feel sorry for you. This is annoying and self-centered. Whiners usually lie about how much they don't have, how life is unfair to them, how their partners and relationships suck, etc.... They exaggerate how bad things are.

Bitches get things done. Whiners wallow in self-pity (oh, poor me!). Whiners make me sick.

34

Everything Is a Process

Everything takes time. Time heals or softens pain.
Time gives you time to make a decision and come
up with a solution. Time should make us SMART-
ER. Unfortunately, people often get themselves
into trouble by making rash and poorly rationalized
decisions. This is poor impulse control.

Some people don't want to hurt their poor little
brains by thinking too much about decisions or the
future. Therefore, they make stupid decisions that
will impact their lives in many negative ways —
i.e., "I'll marry this person that I've known for five
months because he is nice and better than the last
weirdo I latched onto," or "This one drink or line of
cocaine won't hurt me even though I'm in recovery

and a natural-born addict," or "I'll drop out of college because I have to study too much and it's hard." I could give thousands of examples of bad decisions that were not thought through. Most things that are worthwhile are hard!!! Examples are learning to ski well, having a real career, raising good kids, or cooking a gourmet meal; even traveling well is a job that requires effort and thinking.

But even the best-laid plans go awry sometimes, and you need to think of strategies and solutions and backup plans. Plans for recouping or picking up the pieces and starting over or patching relationships TAKE TIME! Everything is a process. We should all reflect on how everything that was difficult in life was a process. It's important to ask, "Is this difficult because I didn't think the decision through?"

35

Forgiveness Is Overrated

I grew up in a middle-class family in mid-America, Ohio. Not an inner city ghetto, but a lovely kind of "Leave It to Beaver" neighborhood. And both of my parents were victims of violent crimes. My father was shot and paralyzed at the age of 55 (I was 21). He sat in a wheelchair for almost 35 years. He died three weeks before his 90th birthday. It was a miracle that he lived that long (most people die a few years after a severe spinal cord injury).

He lived so long because he was the strongest, most courageous, non-whining, funniest human being I have ever met (and I know more people than most). He had three devoted adult children and a good wife. We all took good care of him because we loved him so much and he loved us so much. He never lost his will to live because of his incredible character, humor, and devoted family. He was the most compassionate man in the world, and the toughest.

I learned many things from my father — the most important was to be tough when you need to be tough and extremely compassionate when compassion is needed.

The 21-year-old scumbag who shot Dad in the back (my father owned a car business and was taking him out for a test drive) did only four years in prison for ruining my father's life and stealing his ability to walk for 34 ½ years.

I was a bleeding-heart liberal before my father was shot. After that and 33 years of counseling all kinds of people have made me realize that prison is the best rehab for many scumbag people. But our prisons should be like the horrible ones in foreign countries (no flat screen TV's, ice cream, pool, etc...). They should be so uncomfortable that people would MIND going to prison. Yes, there are people that want to go back to prison because it's better than living on the streets.

All monsters who rape children — especially their own kids — should be lethally injected (just my opinion). That is the most heinous crime on earth.

My mother was molested at 86 years old while recuperating from pneumonia at a very nice nursing home. The molester got only five years in prison.

I have tremendous respect for our penal system now, but it needs to be tougher to deter serious crimes. The epitome of bullshit is the federal judge who ordered state prison officials to provide tax-payer-funded sex-change surgery to a transgender inmate serving life in prison for murdering his wife. I'm a supporter of LGBTQ, but paying for murderers to have this surgery is the kind of thing that is going to be the demise of our society.

I am not saying that forgiveness is a bad thing; it's usually a great character trait except when the "biggies," — rape, murder, incest, etc... — are involved. That's why Catholics differentiate between venial (little) and mortal (big) sins. I hope there is a Higher Power who will dole out the appropriate consequences as well.

36

Put the Fun in Funeral

My next-door neighbor, Coral, whom I adore, recently told me about a eulogy that she wrote and delivered for her dear friend. She said the audience laughed and wanted her to do their eulogies.

She could make the mourners laugh because her friend was funny and kind and only wanted to make others feel good about themselves. He was also smart and snarky (a trait I love).

What do you think people will say about you at your funeral? If you're a serious asshole; people won't be laughing.

Of course we want our loved ones to miss us, but don't you want them to remember you because you made the world a better and funnier place? Not that you created chaos, problems, and bullshit.

If you have done that in your lifetime, you will have a serious funeral and people won't say much about what kind of a person you were because it's not polite to say that he/she was an asshole, drunk, cheater, thief, or someone who was lazy, hateful, jealous, etc....

But that's what they are thinking.

37

Lessons I Learned from My Father

My reflections on the day my dad died:

1) Survive and cope with the adversarial aspects of life with bravery, strength, and dignity.

2) Love family and friends more than anything.

3) Be tough when you need to and extremely compassionate when compassion is needed.

4) The human spirit is real and can overcome the greatest obstacles.

5) Be adventurous and love life.

6) People are more important than things.

7) Tell a really good story and entertain others.

8) Be prudent about money and don't go into debt.

9) Enjoy good food, but enjoy family and friends more.

10) For a parent, love and boundaries are a DELI-CATE BALANCE.

11) Endure physical and emotional pain while still having love in your heart.

38

Meditation Is the Bomb

I was raised Roman Catholic and for six years went to Catholic schools where all students went to Mass every morning. There were some great nuns, but many were what I like to call "Nazi-ninja nuns." They hit you sometimes, wouldn't let you go to the bathroom when you needed to, and made you believe that you were going to burn in purgatory for 1,000 years for having an impure thought or eating meat on Friday.

I rebelled and went to public schools beginning in the seventh grade. I went to a Catholic university but told them I wasn't Catholic so I wouldn't have to take theology. But God must have wanted me to be Catholic because I ended up teaching in Catholic schools about six years in Ohio and Florida.

I actually appreciate my Catholic education now, because we learned more than the public school kids (I didn't have to study for three years in public schools because we had learned it all in Catholic schools). If you survived the mean nuns (not all of them), you developed a wonderful and snarky sense of humor. I can usually spot a product of Catholic education by nuns in anyone over 55 by his or her sense of humor.

I decided to send my daughter to Catholic schools so she could be disciplined/tortured by nuns, too. But by then there were hardly any teaching nuns left in parochial schools. She's very smart and successful in science, probably because she attended an amazing public high school.

I call myself a "cafeteria Catholic." I pick and choose what I like about my cultural faith. But thanks to one of my dearest friends, I have found true spirituality and peace through meditation, specifically raj yoga, which means mind yoga.

I attend meditation sessions nearly every week at my friend's home and learn about being the best person I can be to acquire good karma (grace). I actually sit quietly and think about God and all sorts of good things. It is the most peaceful time of my entire week, and it gets me through all kinds of annoying situations, showing me how to deal with unreasonable and otherwise horrible people that I would like to punch. I have learned to spiritually detach from them.

It always amazes me how psychological theories and practices are based so much on what we learn in meditation. For example, changing our thinking changes our behavior, and that will then change our character. Wow! That's what therapists call cognitive behavioral therapy. Frequently an excellent formula for people needing help is:

Meds + therapy + meditation (spirituality) = stability.

39

The Trick

Here are the tricks to living a good life:

Homeostasis = balance. Balance your life and know your limitations. Have boundaries with yourself and others, and balance family, friends, work, and hobbies. Some days are easier than others to keep in sync. Keep life simple so you can enjoy it and cope with the inevitable stressors, both big and small, that will come almost daily, like "Oh, crap, there's dog poop in the living room!" and "Oh, no! I think I'm having a heart attack."

COPE – don't just survive. Don't freak out about little things, and have convictions about the big stuff. And don't make STUPID decisions.

Have lots of good friends, and kick the bad ones to the curb. Don't hang out with any bad people.

Try to develop a great sense of humor.

Love the people you believe deserve to be loved. Display tremendous gratitude to people who are kind and good to you. And always reciprocate. Frequently get the attention of people who have been kind and generous (not just monetarily) to you, and energetically show your appreciation by giving your time, cheering them up, sitting quietly with them, entertaining them, writing them thank-you notes, and telling them that you love them.

Show people your soul – your character.

Epilogue

Thank you for reading my book. I probably have offended some people by my honesty and humor (lucky for those folks that I lost my chapter on "The Art of Hatred)." Sorry if anything bothered you. My advice is to develop a sense of humor, be more pragmatic, and "roll with it."

My daughter likes to call my advice or suggestions "Patti's Platitudes." I love you, Dr. Zoe.

Editor's Note

The foregoing is a sincere, abrupt at times, forcibly direct representation of a clever, talented woman with whom I have been privileged to counsel unfortunate victims of the vagaries of alcoholism, abusive drug use, and other social potholes that are familiar adjuncts to our society. She is a master of therapy who has helped many of those unfortunates become productive, generous, and happy people.

Her direct style has been an important component of her success. She often laments the failure of gentler approaches to therapy to effect positive results with persons who needed to "hear it like it is." Many benefactors of Patti's approach have become close friends to both of us. I am grateful to her for that. So are they.

Ron Siemer, editor and devoted friend

Notes